D0746372

PHOTO BY FREDERIC OHRINGER

Kathryn Walker, Deborah Offner, Emma Butler and Leora Dana in a scene from the New York production of "Rebel Women." Costumes by Carrie F. Robbins.

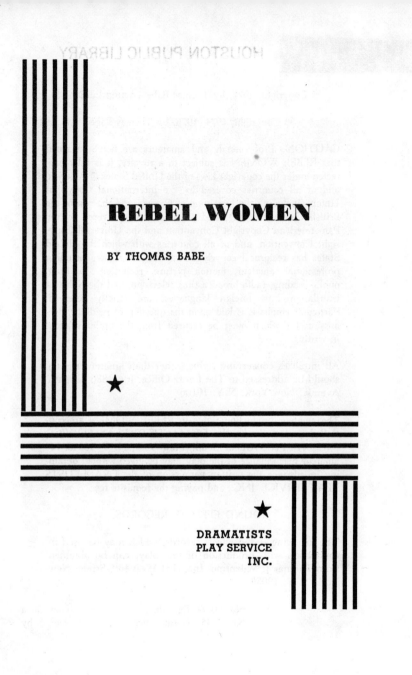

REBEL WOMEN

BY THOMAS BABE

DRAMATISTS
PLAY SERVICE
INC.

R0146818734
HUM

HOUSTON PUBLIC LIBRARY

© Copyright, 1977, by Thomas Babe (Acting Edition)

© Copyright, 1974, 1976, by Thomas Babe

CAUTION: Professionals and amateurs are hereby warned that REBEL WOMEN is subject to a royalty. It is fully protected under the copyright laws of the United States of America, and of all countries covered by the International Copyright Union (including the Dominion of Canada and the rest of the British Commonwealth), and of all countries covered by the Pan-American Copyright Convention and the Universal Copyright Convention, and of all countries with which the United States has reciprocal copyright relations. All rights, including professional, amateur, motion picture, recitation, lecturing, public reading, radio broadcasting, television, and the rights of translation into foreign languages, are strictly reserved. Particular emphasis is laid upon the question of readings, permission for which must be secured from the author's agent in writing.

All inquiries concerning rights (other than amateur rights) should be addressed to The Lantz Office, Inc., 888 Seventh Avenue, New York, N.Y. 10106

The amateur production rights in REBEL WOMEN are controlled exclusively by the DRAMATISTS PLAY SERVICE, INC., 440 Park Avenue South, New York, N. Y. 10016. No amateur performance of the play may be given without obtaining in advance the written permission of the DRAMATISTS PLAY SERVICE, INC., and paying the requisite fee.

SOUND EFFECTS RECORDS

The following sound effects records, which may be used in connection with production of this play, can be obtained from Thomas J. Valentino, Inc., 151 West 46th Street, New York, N.Y. 10036.

No. 5017—Reveille
No. 5045—Cannon fire

REBEL WOMEN was first presented by the New York Shakespeare Festival, Joseph Papp, producer, at the Newman (Public) Theater, in New York City, on June 3, 1976. It was directed by Jack Hofsis; the setting was by John Lee Beatty; costumes were by Carrie B. Robbins; lighting was by Neil Peter Jampolis; music was composed by Catherine MacDonald; lyrics were by Barbara Bonfigli; and the associate producer was Bernard Gersten. The cast, in order of speaking, was as follows:

TUSSIE	Deloris Gaskins
KATHARINE KING	Deborah Offner
MRS. MARY E. LAW	Leora Dana
MRS. MARY LAW ROBARTS	Kathryn Walker
FIRST SOLDIER	Eric Anthony Roberts
SECOND SOLDIER	Mark Kilogi
THIRD SOLDIER/CIVILIAN	David Dean
MAJOR ROBERT STEELE STRONG	Mandy Patinkin
DR. SAMUEL SUTLER	John Glover
GENERAL WILLIAM TECUMSEH SHERMAN	David Dukes
LIEUTENANT HENRY HITCHCOCK	Peter Weller
SOLDIERS	Ralph Byers, Tracey Walter

The summer home of the Law family in Vidalia, Georgia, December 5–6, 1864.

ACT ONE

Late afternoon

ACT TWO

Evening of the same day

ACT THREE

Dawn, the following day

3

CHARACTERS

The family:

MRS. MARY E. LAW, 57, mother, widow, somewhat enfeebled by a
nervous disorder.

MRS. MARY LAW ROBARTS, 27, her daughter, plainly beautiful now
in the mid-days of her pregnancy.

MISS KATE KING, 19, a neighbor and friend, very pretty.

TUSSIE, a black serving woman, middle-aged.

The Federal army:

WILLIAM TECUMSEH SHERMAN, 44, General, with red hair, a
sturdy frame and occasionally that look in the eye which Brady
photographed.

MAJOR ROBERT STEELE STRONG, 28, adjutant to Sherman; his
cheeks are still ruddy and his beard light.

SAMUEL SUTLER, 30s, doctor of philosophy and merchant, handsome and outlandishly dressed.

LIEUTENANT HENRY HITCHCOCK, 20, staff assistant, a good
old boy.

THREE SOLDIERS, very young, black with dirt, coarse.

Other soldiers and civilians and personnel of the Army of the West.

4

NOTE

In the late fall, 1864, hundreds of Georgian families fled Atlanta, anticipating the arrival of General William Sherman and his Union forces. Ordinarily, these land-owning families would have spent the winter in the city, but instead, they moved back to their just-closed country homes, hoping to avoid the path of Sherman's march. On November 16th, Sherman, having taken Atlanta, left it a smouldering ruins and headed for the sea, 250 miles to the east.

For

Julia Clark Boak

REBEL WOMEN

ACT ONE

The setting, which remains the same throughout, is a large living room with adjacent grand hall, staircase and the suspicion of other rooms and alcoves in the large summer home of the Law family, Vidalia, Georgia, at the end of the year, 1864. The room is elegantly appointed, but uncluttered, even bare, seemingly vast. There is evidence that some things have been taken down, packed up, hidden. Several large French windows opening onto a gallery invite us to see the damp, gray, cold winter outside, a landscape nonetheless illumined from time to time during the action by brilliant skies and piercing sunlight. We also have the feeling of dense vegetation, of a suffocating woefulness which the land for the most part reflects, embodies. Outside the windows and doors, mostly out of sight, throughout the action, much happens: people come and go, walking, in wagons, on horseback; there are explosions; we see traces of fire and smoke in the sky; horses and men wait around impatiently; weird military music, out of whack; crying and wailing; shouts; singing; laughter; bathing in a trough; the noise of chickens, ducks, geese, cattle; the crash of a wall of logs falling; a hammer on an anvil; gunshots; more laughter, then more and more laughter, too much of it; then, finally, the sound of nothing; reveille. Now it is late in the afternoon; high tea is concluding. Mrs. Law, Kate King, Tussie and Mary all present, sorting through the belongings they have brought with them from Atlanta. Bombardment without, which punctuates their speech.

MRS. ROBARTS. (*Sing-song.*)
Butcher, barker, virtue's thief,
Banker, lawyer, army chief.

7

MRS. LAW. We simply will not concern ourselves with this Sherman.

TUSSIE. Amen.

KATE. They're all frightful little boys, but I do think they'll be of use to us, in some way, I don't know how. (*Explosion.*) Now that's not more than a mile off. See, I told you, I told you!

MRS. LAW. What cannot be helped must be endured.

MRS. ROBARTS. They burned his church, too, did you hear? My husband's church. The blue-bellied sons of bitches.

MRS. LAW. Mary, I must ask you.

KATE. Well, I think I'd do anything for a taste of their company.

MRS. ROBARTS. Who?

KATE. Men.

MRS. ROBARTS. You are a foolish thing, Kate King, is there anybody in the world, I wonder, who doesn't know that? Three days ago these Lincolnite soldiers under Sherman arrived in Roswell, oh, you remember what a tiny, peaceful place that Roswell was. Five hundred women, old, young, black, white, comely, pitted and scarred, working peacefully in the two big mills, spinning cotton for uniforms and bedclothes and bandages. Well, Sherman arrested every one of them and after peaceful Roswell was pillaged and burned to the ground before their eyes, the women were loaded, five hundred of them, into railway freight cars and shipped North, declared criminal traitors. Some died outright, naturally; some suffered nervous collapses and will never recover. Others just fell quiet and stared at each other hopelessly as the dusty, turd-strewn cars travelled North over a hard roadbed lambasted by shell. I know all about that. I dreamed about it last night, riding with them. When I think about it, I am so shaking with rage I can hardly be still a moment.

KATE. (*Rushing to comfort her.*) Dearest Mary, please, think of the child; think of health. This is a civilized world and these men are part of it. (*Mary looks out the window.*)

MRS. ROBARTS. They're here, three soldiers in blue uniforms, I can make out just three, coming slowly towards us. Can we do anything?

MRS. LAW. Sit there, my dear child. I'll attend to these *soi-disant* conquerors.

KATE. They're ever so ugly, aren't they, giants? They must be from Ohio. I think I shall faint dead away.

8

MRS. LAW. Stop it this minute, both of you, do you hear me?

MRS. ROBARTS. Sit close, Kate, I feel a chill. (*Soldiers enter.*)

SOLDIER ONE. Why didn't you answer when we knocked on your door? We can burn down your goddamn house and everything in it if you don't respond to our lawful summons, did you know that?

MRS. LAW. I was unaware.

SOLDIER ONE. You got any firearms?

MRS. LAW. No.

SOLDIER ONE. Not so much as a goddamn butcher knife?

MRS. LAW. A butcher knife is not a firearm.

SOLDIER ONE. Is that so? Do you have any silver?

SOLDIER TWO. Where do you keep your wine. We met some men down the road and they said they got some wine offen you and two jugs of rye, so you better look smart and not lie to us, you hear, you old rebel whore?

MRS. LAW. Would you permit any man to speak like that to your mother or your wife?

SOLDIER TWO. None of us got wives. (*They think this is funny.*)

SOLDIER ONE. Where's your silver?

MRS. LAW. You are not entitled under the general articles of war to entail non-combatant civilians in a hostile country.

SOLDIER ONE. I wonder if Uncle Billy knows that. I reckon he wrote the rules and he says if you lying rebel whores don't answer your doors then you're to be made an example of and we'll do it. Now that's all written down, you understand?

SOLDIER THREE. (*Conciliatory, ingratiating.*) If you deal fairly with us, see, and tell the truth, then we'll put up this here special providential conduct notice that says you've been placed under Federal protection and no soldier from here to Atlanta or back will dare bother you, and it's signed by General Sherman hisself, at Lincoln's bidding.

MRS. ROBARTS. Do it, Mama.

MRS. LAW. (*To Mary.*) Hush, we're being fooled. No such commission exists, to my knowledge.

SOLDIER ONE. Where's the silver? We have to make an inventory.

MRS. LAW. Do what you want but I won't help you. I know the

9

general articles of war and even Mr. Lincoln knows them. So do what you want. I know.

SOLDIER TWO. We're instructed to forage, but alls we want is a little wine.

MRS. LAW. No.

SOLDIER TWO. Well, shit! (*Silence. The soldiers put their heads together, then withdraw. Soldier Two busts a vase on the way out. They are gone.*)

MRS. LAW. (*Finally, flatly.*) It was wholly unnecessary to break that vase. It was a vulgar and gratuitous assertion of will.

KATE. I was afraid, I was truly afraid.

MRS. LAW. Behave yourself, Kate. Don't affect to be so flighty. Mary?

MRS. ROBARTS. I'm all right, Mother. I'm much better than I thought I was going to be. In fact, I think I liked their finally being there, for a moment at least.

MRS. LAW. They may come or they may go, but we will hew to our business. (*Explosion.*)

KATE. They are making a great deal more commotion than is necessary, in my opinion. And why did they have to destroy all the roads and railroads and the telegraph? I want to know more from Atlanta, from my poor mama, now that she's alone. Oh, dear.

MRS. LAW. Now, Kate, she's safe enough. We know that from her letter. And you're safe enough here, for now. We must dig in.

MRS. ROBARTS. This war they are making is on women, it's come down to that finally. A few strong men who think we aren't. Sally Douglas wrote me from Roswell that one would have thought, when the gallant Yanks came to town, that it was a celebration, a festival of bastards, she said, ruffians tearing through her house, their mouths filled with cursing and bitterness and the damnedest lies about slavery. When my husband left us before tea this afternoon to take those tired mules to Mrs. Rush Wilson, I thought, well, Reverend Robarts, if they intercept you, a man, at some crossroads, be sure they will shoot you or hang you or feed you to the lions. But we, sir, when they find us, we shall be toyed with and they will ask us politely for what they don't really want, then take outright what is **never mentioned.** These very clear pictures of it invade my thoughts, Mama, and I can't help it, I'm sorry.

MRS. LAW. You are like your father, Mary. When he was—it must have been all of 27 years of age, he and I attended the Independence Day festival in Roswell. Those were grand events then, and they used to place a great charge of gunpowder under the smithy's anvil and ignite it, and the anvil was blown with a dreadful roar twenty feet into the air. It was their way of celebration, the men, but your father was innocent of the event that day and when the explosion came, he looked startled, clutched his breast and cried, "I am shot, I die!" We were so frightened for him, but it was just his nervous imaginings. Just before he died three years ago, he wrote me in a letter from Atlanta: "Did you know, Elizabeth, this is the first night I've slept out of your company in 32 years, and I find it wounds my spirit, it does." We were so close for so long that we rather became one another and you would have had trouble disentangling us. When I dream at all now, it is of him, your father, standing among us with a book in his hand, the only book I think, and I am sitting by in astonishment, asking only if it is time yet for me to join him. (*Explosion.*)

KATE. I don't see why we left the city to endure this. When they burned Atlanta, I wonder, did they burn Dr. Brace Hartley's surgery? (*Pause.*) And why wouldn't he settle here, when he had the chance, when there was such an opportunity? It was a judgment against him that he thought he was too good for us and had to betake himself to Atlanta to be with the wonderful young women who lived there, who dance so well. I wonder. We met at the June social when the first peaches had just been picked. You remember that? Young Mr. Marcus Stephenson preached so movingly? I was thirteen and it was the first time I was visited with the maiden's curse. I felt so bitter and lost. The strain kept getting wider and would it ever stop I wondered? Well, I don't know why I'm recalling a peach social, whether it was Dr. Hartley and the ice cream he proferred, or the harvest of all the trees we were able to get then, or whether I saw that things had changed so inutterably, had gotten so heavy, so that my heart broke and I cried and I didn't know why, except that I wanted someone to put his arm around my shoulder that day. Well, I thought that was the end of the world then, can you imagine? And now I remember everything, it seems the happiest time of my life, and I wish I could feel completely, and sufficiently sad again about a dish of cold ice cream. (*Pause; brightly.*) It's no fun, that's all, being a young thing, solo, at nineteen in Georgia just at this time of this particular year.

MRS. ROBARTS. But I'm 27, and carrying a child, four months

11

into it. Why is that Kate? Mother, do you know why it is that I am carrying a child? I should want to know why.

MRS. LAW. You'll know the answer, dear, in time. (*The familiar sounds of boots on the porch, a knock, silence. Major Strong and Dr. Samuel Sutler enter.*)

STRONG. How do you do? Do I have the honor of addressing the owner of the house?

MRS. LAW. You do.

STRONG. I am Major Robert Steele Strong, United States Army and I have the obligation to inform you that your house has been commandeered by the Army of the West, William T. Sherman, commander, for purposes of temporary headquarters and hospital for said army. You will be compensated for such viands and other supplies as we may have occasion to use. May I assume that you have understood me and that even if you would wish it otherwise, you will not feel aggrieved at what we have been compelled by necessity to ask?

MRS. LAW. You are safe in assuming that I have understood.

STRONG. Just so. (*Pause, which is awkward for everyone.*)

KATE. Is there anything you want . . . immediately?

STRONG. No.

MRS. LAW. Will you sit?

STRONG. No.

SUTLER. I will, thank you.

MRS. ROBARTS. Would you . . .

SUTLER. Ma'am?

MRS. ROBARTS. Would you brush some of the dust from your coat before you sit down. (*Pause.*) I'm sorry. What a foolish punctillio. Mrs. Robarts be still.

SUTLER. Not at all. I have an appreciation for your sensibilities. None of us like this much, you know.

MRS. ROBARTS. But that's simply not true. Some of you love it very much. It is an incarnation.

SUTLER. I don't know. (*Pause.*)

KATE. Shall I make some tea, then?

MRS. LAW. No, I think not. We've had our tea. It is time to batten down for the night. Tussie, would you see that the dishes are removed now?

TUSSIE. Yes ma'am.

MRS. LAW. Thank you. Could you tell me, Major, how much of

12

my house you are constrained to commandeer? I grow tired easily these days.

STRONG. I'm sorry, I can't, but wherever you go, if you must sleep, we'll consider that inviolate. The same with . . . uh . . .

MRS. ROBARTS. Mrs. Robarts, a poor gentlewoman.

KATE. And Kate King. We can go anywhere, then, almost as if you weren't here?

STRONG. You are confined, of course. You will be, whiles we are here. I have no reason to doubt of you personally, but some women in your position—and I by no means imply that this is in your natures—would gladly reveal our headquarters location to guerrillas or cavalry operating behind our lines.

MRS. ROBARTS. Oh, you are too much, Major. I shall have to try hard to be afraid of you.

STRONG. (*Uncomfortable.*) I hope so.

SUTLER. But if I can be of service . . . ?

MRS. LAW. I think not.

KATE. How?

MRS. LAW. I think not.

SUTLER. If you need anything. I am a merchant and I am allowed to trade a little, to aid gentlewomen in distress. I will take anything in exchange.

MRS. ROBARTS. A mercenary, vulturous pimp. We must have these in our house, too? We must turn our house into this?

SUTLER. You have the wrong idea, I fear. I am only doing the job which I know, and which the creator designated for me. If I did not . . . trade . . . there would be someone else, of course, but he might be less humane and rational than I am, less attractive. You see that, don't you?

MRS. ROBARTS. Someone must have us, and you will be nice about it.

SUTLER. I was saying that, yes. You are very quick-witted.

MRS. ROBARTS. Please, Mr. . . .

SUTLER. Sutler, Dr. Samuel Sutler.

MRS. ROBARTS. Doctor?

SUTLER. Of philosophy.

MRS. ROBARTS. (*Unable to stifle her laughter.*) Oh, where will this grotesque comedy take us, Dr. Samuel Sutler, do you have any idea?

MRS. LAW. Mary, perhaps you should not agitate yourself.

13

MRS. ROBARTS. I cannot help myself.

KATE. And you say the General himself will come here?

STRONG. Tonight.

KATE. Oh dear, I think that is terribly exciting.

MRS. ROBARTS.

Butcher, barker, virtues thief,
Banker, lawyer, Army's chief.

KATE. And what is he, that he is, that he comes here spoken of so fearfully?

MRS. LAW. Kate King, have you no shame at all?

SUTLER. As God is my witness, William Tecumseh Sherman is the most remarkable man that this remarkable sectional upheaval has elevated. He has written his name large in his grand strategy. Sherman's march to the sea began 22 days ago, and before him, white men flee and Negras flock, singing the day of Jubilo done come. Truly, we have learned to read a fiery gospel at his behest. Food, livestock and the ancestral relics of the South are plundered alike; you see privates dressed up in ball gowns on every flank. But it's okay, as Matty Van B. was fond of opining: they're not forcing white women, no sir. Those broad-backed Johnnies are coupling with Negresses in the dark around every campfire and colored concubines are riding wagons already groaning under the weight of stolen hams, beef, sorghum, and sweet potatoes. Not a life has been taken nor atrocity performed by this man, but I have seen his troopers destroy a railroad with hot vengeance, wrapping incandescent rails around white pines and twisting them into the letters U.S. When Cump Sherman got his horse between his legs in Atlanta and pointed eastwards, he rode down lines and lines of boys with hardly a pair of peanuts in their pants—and they whispered in a voice he could hear— "Well, Uncle Billy, I guess Grant is waiting for us in Richmond."

MRS. ROBARTS. And nonsense to you, dear doctor. (*The commotion of the troops, arriving.*)

STRONG. They're here. If you would be so good as to excuse me ladies. (*Exits.*)

SUTLER. That Strong's a good boy, watch him, but he's an awful pain in the tail, if you'll excuse me.

KATE. Really?

MRS. LAW. (*Suddenly, apprehensive.*) Well, I don't want to meet anyone more. I see no reason to. (*She goes to leave just as Sher-*

man, several aides, Strong and Hitchcock all appear. The room is engulfed with activity.) Excuse me. (*She is ignored.*) Excuse me!

SHERMAN. (*Slightly annoyed.*) What is it?

MRS. LAW. Shall we be expected to do anything for you?

SHERMAN. Do anything?

MRS. LAW. Will there be any demands?

SHERMAN. Does anyone have any idea what this woman is talking about or why she should be standing there, molesting me?

STRONG. This is her house.

SHERMAN. Well, it is a nice house, one of the nicer ones I've seen. I hope it comes to no harm. (*Pause, notices all the women for the first time.*) Go on now, no one will hurt you.

MRS. LAW. I must say that your decency becomes you.

SHERMAN. Is that so?

MRS. ROBARTS. Well, I am nearly bored to tears with being terrified of this man, this beast here. How do you do, General? My name is Mary Law Robarts.

SHERMAN. How do you do, Mrs. Robarts?

MRS. ROBARTS. This is Kathrine King.

SHERMAN. How do you do, Miss King?

MRS. ROBARTS. And she is also pleased to meet you, and the Major, and everybody, but she, like the rest of us, is constrained to hate you.

SHERMAN. That's the color of things, Mrs. Robarts. No one is sorrier than myself.

MRS. ROBARTS. I don't think so.

MRS. LAW. Mary, if you would be so good, dear.

MRS. ROBARTS. This man is obviously a hypocrite. He exhibits a false piety about the way in which he happens to earn his living.

MRS. LAW. Mary, the General's philosophy is essentially alien and you will only demean yourself by making yourself available to him.

MRS. ROBARTS. For 3 years I've wanted to make my stand, like this, because I've been so confined, *ma mere*, so wretchedly pent up.

SHERMAN. I must say that hostility is not unfamiliar to me, though I think most of it is ill-directed. It is occasionally salutory to vent some degree of rage, but I am not bound, Mrs. Robarts, to be a witness. I am sorry for what you imagine to be depredations to your person, my hypocrisies, and so forth. The purposes of

15

mankind, I mean the best purposes, will generally be served by what you call my way of making a living, my victories. I can appreciate that you have difficulty in seeking that at the moment.

MRS. ROBARTS. (*Quoting.*) "In the midst of peace and prosperity, it was the South who dared and badgered us to battle, insulted our flag, seized our arsenals and forts, expelled Union families by the thousand, burned their houses. To be sure. I have made war vindictively; war is war and you can make nothing else of it; but if we must be enemies, let us be men and fight it out as we propose to do, and not deal in hypocritical appeals to God and humanity."

SHERMAN. (*Startled.*) It is not enough that you have read my letter; you have committed it to memory exactly.

MRS. ROBARTS. There is little to do this season in Georgia. You *are* talked about, General.

SHERMAN. But I take it you are not persuaded, Mrs. Robarts?

MRS. ROBARTS. Good heavens, no. I can understand a pettifogger trying to justify himself by saying all those hard-hearted things, those big, strong, muscular phrases about war, but General, you appear to have some delicacy and needn't be afraid to show it before me. War is war. Really!

SHERMAN. War is hell.

MRS. ROBARTS. More muscular still.

SHERMAN. I make no pretense to understand the feminine mentality.

MRS. ROBARTS. Why do you say such a thing, such an empty old wheeze. I'm more of a man than you in some ways, and you have some of the delicacy and charm of a woman, something about the attention you pay in spite of yourself.

SHERMAN. I'm sure I don't know what the hell you're talking about. Is she deranged?

MRS. LAW. I warned you. Now this graceful and cultured soldier has concluded that you are no more than a loonie.

MRS. ROBARTS. I don't think so, no; rather I think he's puzzled.

SHERMAN. Perhaps we could discuss this another time . . . uh, anything you've a mind to?

MRS. ROBARTS. Perhaps, but I must save my strength, you know.

SHERMAN. Yes, your condition is delicate, I have taken note.

MRS. LAW. We'll not bother you.

MRS. ROBARTS. (*They make to exit, Mary returns with a hint*

16

of desperation.) General, I must say— I'll never have another chance— I must say this situation, all of it, the way it's dragged on and befouled us, so that we, none of us, are ourselves, can't have ourselves be— (*Pause. Anger at peak.*) you must be told. You have violated us, you have forced us to know you. You are a species of rapist, and yet you have no passion at all, no lechery. (*Pause.*) Well, I have said that and it doesn't seem to make any difference. I am sorry to have gone so far in.

SHERMAN. You've asked this on yourselves. I have only little problems to solve, nothing of policy. You make war and I must break the will to make that war. Therefore, I purposefully demoralize every man, woman and child in this bloody land. Your crops will vanish, your animals, your houses, every last shred of sustenance until it is so excruciating to continue to make war that you will stop, you will cease altogether. That much is simple. I have no passion for war, you're correct; I am a man with a very specific mission, a problem, very specific in lineaments and I do not foam at the mouth, no, truly, nor will I, over poor Georgia protrate, her will shattered. Mr. Lincoln did not choose me for any such loose sentiments I might have. I appreciate what I am doing is painful; that is it's purpose. But I lack the anger, the malice aforethought, and I am proud of this deficiency.

MRS. ROBARTS. But you are actively malicious, a thing I find corrupt. Well, this is total war, Sherman, all parts rendered. I feel certain my mother's house will have to burn, otherwise we will think we have won the day, and our morale will not be sufficiently cracked.

MRS. LAW. I will not apologize for my daughter, although she is overwrought. It is not manly for you to tease her and ply her and draw her out. Pray, have some regard for our dignities.

SHERMAN. I think I wanted my position—well, who in God's name knows now whether I can say anything till the heat's gone out of it. I am not incapable of feeling sorrow for her, the wretch, for the South. I loved her while I lived among you.

MRS. ROBARTS. Please contain this overflowing.

SHERMAN. It exists nonetheless. (*Pause.*) I admire you, that is, your courage.

MRS. ROBARTS. But you concede nothing?

SHERMAN. What?

MRS. ROBARTS. You do not concede?

17

SHERMAN. Christ on the bloody cross, take her away, take her out of my presence. Now, take her!

MRS. ROBARTS. (*Cold, steely voice.*) He means to hurt us, quite deeply.

SHERMAN. Strong, if they will not, Strong, at once remove, you, Strong, will aid them, Strong. With compassionate force you will see that she is gone, Strong. This is unnatural, truly!

MRS. ROBARTS. Oh, my! (*Laughing uncertainly.*)

STRONG. I must ask you . . .

MRS. LAW. We'll go of course. This is a most uncertain thing, General, this business, what you do, how we must be. Most uncertain, very disturbing. (*The women, all except Kate King, exit. She goes to her trunk.*)

SHERMAN. Goddamnit! (*Throws clipboard down.*) It's nothing. Strong, where's the whiskey? Hitchcock, would you be good enough to have Davis, Williams and Osterhaus all arrange to have representatives of their commands here tomorrow morning. I don't care how much bellyaching there is about hard rides and guerillas, I don't give a good goddamn. We're going to get done with this, goddamnit to hell!

HITCHCOCK. Yes sir. (*Exits.*)

SUTLER. Miss King?

KATE. Yes sir?

SUTLER. You are distressed for Mrs. Robarts?

KATE. No. Well, naturally . . .

SUTLER. But something distresses you?

KATE. How perceptive. I feel I must have something. I'm like a child, really.

SUTLER. What must you have?

KATE. My happiness, just like a baby. Gifts, music, cool nights in the spring. Why should I think of that, I wonder, especially when Mrs. Robarts has left us with so many important things to think about.

SUTLER. You think what she said was important? You, personally, I mean?

KATE. Why, yes, don't you?

SUTLER. Not much. There was a mote too much morality about it.

KATE. Of course, I didn't follow every word.

SUTLER. Too much Ten-Commanding.

KATE. Yes, but one mustn't kill, mustn't steal, mustn't commit
. . . the so-forths, do you think so?

SUTLER. I'm a businessman and a certain amount of my work,
alas, is stealing. I do indeed covet my neighbors ass, if not his man-
servant: that's my ambition. Killing, I think, for strictly policy
reasons, should be limited. As for the worship of false gods, rever-
ing mothers and fathers, adultery—filling, all of it, to get the number up to ten.

KATE. My, aren't you cynical and worldly, just wonderful, and
you smell of the horse you've been riding this very day. I must tell
you I am not without substance of my own.

SUTLER. I can appreciate that, my dear young woman. But there
are differences . . .

KATE. And you do romance; you're in a kind of romance business.

SUTLER. No, but you can think I'm handsome if you want, with
these eyes of mine: they *are* handsome, but they're more reading
glasses than—what shall we say—*objets d'art*? Still, fall in love if
you wish; it's a kind of romance business and I do have *my* needs.

KATE. You are conceited, but with reason, I suppose. But I believe
you ought to flatter me, too, not just yourself, especially if we are
to get anywhere.

SUTLER. Where are we going? I didn't know.

KATE. It seemed to me, well, say I have a kind face, soft hair,
because some hair is very coarse, you know, or that my form is as
a form ought to be, comely. I want to be spoken well of, before
anything else is well done by me.

SUTLER. You outrageous little slut!

KATE. That's not the compliment I had in mind, dear doctor.
Lord, Lord, this war is drawing down the value of things. You are
not subtle, Sutler, do you appreciate me?

SUTLER. I feel sure we can come to terms. I have danced a great
deal from Chattanooga to here, especially while Cump Sherman
called the tune—and even he knows how well he calls the tune,
how he loves the dance. It seems to me we have been lewd as spar-
rows, twenty-two days at least, and it is called by the correspon-
dents and some others a war. I have danced a good deal indeed, and
I may take the next turn with you, if your card is not full.

KATE. I have to be won, you know, my heart must be won with
dignity.

SUTLER. Call it what you want, there's a chance for fun. I don't

19

feel oppressed by things, no, dear lady, but some of these people: all thunder-fire in the cane break and the name of God himself!

KATE. General Sherman?

SUTLER. I don't concern myself, truly. I'm an educated man. He went to West Point. He's entitled to take things hard.

KATE. I tend to take things hard.

SUTLER. (*Uncertain.*) Is that true? And you seem so frivolous.

KATE. (*Anguished.*) Oh, dear, you've gone too far!

SUTLER. Gracious Peter! Take some pride in being of no consequence. Things are the simplier thereby.

KATE. (*Puzzled.*) Are you, at last, trying to flatter me?

SHERMAN. (*Another theatrical outburst.*) Who is he? Who's written this stuff? I'll have him buried to his eyes in ants. Strong, why wasn't I told that some horse's ass has introduced a bill in the Congress to prevent me or any other modern Attila—it says here—from foraging wantonly off the land.

STRONG. I don't know, sir. But I don't think such a measure will curry much favor.

SHERMAN. No? Maybe you know something about politics that I don't.

STRONG. You are a consummate politician, if I may say.

SHERMAN. You mayn't. Don't be a boot-licker, Strong, never.

STRONG. I wasn't sir. That was an ironic compliment, knowing what you think of politicians. But I admire you.

SHERMAN. I don't like irony.

STRONG. I think you know, sir, that you are widely admired, very widely loved?

SHERMAN. Truth to tell. Not by the South, by God.

STRONG. Not openly.

SHERMAN. (*Amused, with warmth.*) Well, heaven protect the armies of the West and their humble Coriolanus. You think all this is proper, Strong?

STRONG. What, sir?

SHERMAN. Being loved, very widely loved, to use your words, by soldiers? I don't need that compliment, if it is a compliment, that contaminant. A few of them are going to die and more than a few are going to be God-Almighty chewed up, to be certain. So, to love me?

STRONG. They're very immature, General. They've just been from home, most of them and they're used to paying intimate deference to the one who tells them when to get up and when to lie down and where to go and when to die and how.

SHERMAN. I don't accept that doctrine. There is no one more immature in the whole West than yourself, and can you say you love me? I don't understand your muddling about, I'm bound.

STRONG. I'm on a different footing. I've seen a little more of things. But I understand how it may be—

SHERMAN. What is all of this, Strong? My father died when I was six years old, an event of melancholy caste. There was a protracted quiet in our house; I was sure my poor mother would die of it, and afterwards, because we were not well prepared for, I had to live with a step-father, away from family. We were hopelessly scattered across Ohio. So, you might say, I am not disposed to understand your doctrine, and if I did understand it, I would have no feel for it, no need, not in the least, I assure you. To be a soldier, I think, is the best thing on earth.

STRONG. It may be, but I know I'm going to run in the other direction as soon as Lee surrenders, and that's my word.

SHERMAN. Strong, don't tell me what you'd rather. Do something military and useful, like attending to the surgeons reports, which are four days in arrears. How can I know if I have an able-bodied man left?

STRONG. (*Hurt.*) The reports are in order, sir; they have been all along.

SHERMAN. Oh? Oh, well, don't stand there, man, looking on with such—

STRONG. Affection?

SHERMAN. Bloody inquisition. I shall demonstrate no leniency in my dealings. (*Pause.*) Will you have a whiskey, though?

STRONG. Yes sir. (*He pours two drinks, Sherman takes one and walks to window.*)

SHERMAN. You know Strong, Grant runs in a narrower compass than me. I'm smarter than he is by a damn-sight, we both know that; I see into things. But what I see very often frightens me, and he doesn't give a good goddamn. I am a brilliant tactician, but he is certain, even when he's wrong, and I admire him for that. He just goes on.

STRONG. Yes, sir.

SHERMAN. (*Warm.*) And did you know, I used to be a lawyer

21

like yourself, can you imagine, the Tamburlaine of Tennessee, Atlanta's Attila? But I never went to Harvard.

STRONG. Where did you go?

SHERMAN. I was admitted to the bar in a state that had no requirements, save quickness, a new state with aspirations. They needed lawyers more than law, at the moment. (*Pause.*) Well, Strong, tell me something, something Hitchcock doesn't know.

STRONG. He knows everything.

SHERMAN. I don't want gossip. I want some divertissement. I love light entertainment.

STRONG. Really?

SHERMAN. Dancing, the Theatre.

STRONG. I am reading a work by Miss Jane Austen.

SHERMAN. Who is that? An abolitionist? It's not literature.

STRONG. An English authoress.

SHERMAN. Yes, well, never mind, our tastes differ. I love Shakespeare.

STRONG. Do you think that's proper?

SHERMAN. What do you mean?

STRONG. To love Shakespeare, to very widely love Shakespeare, to use my words.

SHERMAN. Oh, I see. Well, now that you shake a stick at it, I'm not sure. Ben Johnson loved Shakespeare and that never got him fried, did it? You're a horsefly, Strong, just dead wrong for the military. Never mind.

STRONG. My father died when I was eight, as I recall, so perhaps that is something we have in common. And the silence that followed, too, though I remained with my mother. What is different is that it was my unhappy chance to be the one who found him, sitting against a tree near the house, with a great hole in his ear where he'd shot himself. (*Pause.*) Impecunity. Infidelity. Incalculable woes of some kind, all very quiet. He was a lumber dealer, very rich, very hard, far away. A philandering petit thief, you would say, who attempted to plant a generation of heroes behind him. Of which I am chief example. Or perhaps you, sir.

SHERMAN. Me? I never knew the man. You have weird precepts, Strong. Still I'm sorry your sorry progenitor was such a woeful and sorry coward.

STRONG. I don't know that he was.

SHERMAN. Really? Well that much seems obvious, Strong. An-

22

other whiskey? (*He pours.*) Why is it always so Goddamn thick about six in the evening down here? You can't sleep, you can't think, you can't manage a Goddamn thing. (*The faint sound of an instrument seems to come from upstairs, and the General looks to investigate.*) Strong, see here, that woman is coming again, the one who's unhinged. Do you think we could avoid her? I don't want to stir her up again, but I can't have her wandering here and there demoralizing everyone with her morbid opinions.

STRONG. Ignore her, sir.

SHERMAN. Well, let me pretend to work. (*Pause.*) Strong, I swear to you I am humiliated to pretend to work to preserve that poor wretched woman's sanity.

STRONG. I'll do what I can sir.

SHERMAN. Thank you, Strong. (*They both pretend to work. Mrs. Robarts opens the door to enter room and retrieve Kate, who has fallen asleep on the sofa.*)

MRS. ROBARTS. Katharine? Dear, are you asleep, dear? You mustn't sleep there dear, you'll be stiff. Wake up, dear. Kate?

KATE. (*Stirring.*) Oh, dear. I have compromised myself and fallen asleep among the enemy.

MRS. ROBARTS. No, no, these gentlemen were too busy with their commerce and their killing to take any notice.

SUTLER. (*Annoyed.*) Most unfair.

KATE. The doctor is not the man you think he is.

MRS. ROBARTS. I'm sure. We really should do nothing precipitous. It is not quite seemly for us to spend too much time among these types of men. Mother and I have withdrawn to an apartment above where we feel certain we won't be bothered. You must join us. We must barricade the door.

KATE. Well, I will, of course. I didn't mean to fall asleep. I was feeling sad the way one does, and the doctor was kind enough to offer me a soothing word.

MRS. ROBARTS. Exactly!

KATE. Let me say goodnight to the doctor.

MRS. ROBARTS. (*Holding her back.*) Say it.

KATE. I want to go over and say it to him.

MRS. ROBARTS. Say it from here.

KATE. I can, but it wouldn't be so pleasant.

MRS. ROBARTS. Kate, I will not let go of you.

KATE. (*Strained.*) Goodnight, Dr. Sutler.

SUTLER. Yes, dear Kate, we'll go over everything later.

MRS. ROBARTS. There will be no more "laters," doctor, if you are a doctor.

SUTLER. Of philosophy.

MRS. ROBARTS. Which means lover of wisdom, doctor. (*Accusingly.*) You are a lover of wisdom!

SUTLER. I can't see that I've harmed you, Mrs. Robarts.

MRS. ROBARTS. You are in this house.

SUTLER. Yes, I am.

MRS. ROBARTS. You are in my house.

SUTLER. Yes.

MRS. ROBARTS. You are in my house. (*To Strong.*) You are in my house, my mother's house! (*To Sherman.*) You are in my mother's house, drunk!

SHERMAN. (*In spite of himself.*) I am not—

MRS. ROBARTS. You are not what? What do you think you are not, Sherman? In my mother's house? Drunk? What have you done to her? Just look. And what about my mother and me? What are you not, Sherman?

SHERMAN. I am not happy about this.

MRS. ROBARTS. Next you will take off your boots in here, and use my father's shaving mirror and later on you will be singing, you and him and all of you.

STRONG. Mrs. Robarts—

MRS. ROBARTS.
    Butcher, barker, virtue's thief,
    Banker, lawyer, army chief . . .

SHERMAN. The last line is more or less accurate. I've been in all those lines of work, some with more success. The rest of it is wholly wrong, churlish.

KATE. I want to tell you, Dr. Sutler, that it is all in the nature of things, do you understand?

SUTLER. I do.

KATE. But it is, do you know what I mean? I have to go.

SUTLER. I understand.

MRS. ROBARTS. (*To Strong.*) You, will you help me get this poor creature out of here and away from this peddler of commercial wisdom.

SUTLER. I have truly done nothing to harm you.

SHERMAN. Stay where you are, Strong.

24

STRONG. Sir?

SHERMAN. That request for your favor is in the general form of an order, Strong. We are all being manipulated for histrionic effect by this charming woman.

KATE. (*Apprehensive.*) I think we'd better go.

MRS. ROBARTS. No, we won't go until I'm certain.

KATE. Oh, he's talking. Everyone knows Yankees are big talkers.

SHERMAN. My wife once wanted me to leave California because she was not happy there and missed her parents. She is a plain woman, by her own admission, but that is of more concern to her than to me. Yet that day she said to me: You deserve something better, she said, a smart splendid woman you can shape to your ends. I am nothing. Let me go. I was entirely and properly moved by what she said, and her confessions of plainness especially touched me. As a consequence, we left. I lost a good business chance, we returned to nothing, we were not measurably better. I mention this anecdote apropos of the way in which my natural feelings have been played upon in the past and as a warning that I have since resolved never to be so pliable again.

MRS. ROBARTS. So your wife is plain, Sherman, but thinks you ought to have some smart, splendid woman to shape to your purposes?

SHERMAN. That was incidental to what I was saying.

MRS. ROBARTS. It is everything, you demented toad, you butcher, well you can't have us, you barker!

SHERMAN. I don't think I want anything, but to finish up and go home.

MRS. LAW. (*Entering.*) Excuse me. Mary, there is a gentleman here who says that your husband, the Reverend Mr. Robarts has been captured and detained by Federal soldiers. I don't know on what grounds. I can't quite make it out.

MRS. ROBARTS. Poor Freddy!

MRS. LAW. Apparently they believe that the Reverend Mr. Robarts is a guerilla or a bushwacker, or alternately, that because such guerillas and bushwackers exist, ordinary people are to be rounded up as hostages, and when one of them is killed from ambush, then one of us will be executed in cold blood. Do I have that policy correctly, General, is that how your order reads?

SHERMAN. In substance.

MRS. LAW. I thought that was how you meant it. In any event, there's nothing we can do about it at the moment. They won't shoot Mr. Robarts tonight, otherwise they wouldn't have allowed for him to send for his Bible and Communion set, don't you think? We shouldn't worry too much until tomorrow, for I believe he will be tried before a proper military court and released according to the older and fairer rules of war. (*Leading her daughter off, out of room, Kate and Jussie following.*) It will be so awful if he is killed, I know that, but we must see what will be decided for us. You shouldn't cry so much for him yet. You shouldn't cry so much for yourself. (*Surprised.*) Are you crying for yourself? (*Women start to exit, freeze, continue, lights fade.*)

ACT TWO

Nine P.M. that evening. The room is quite cluttered and furniture has been moved about the room. Soldiers have taken possession, and Hitchcock sits C., having his hair cut. Major Strong is on the portico, speaking with a Southern civilian.

STRONG. All right, now take this paper to the small agglomeration of white tents, and they'll give you two pounds flour, one pound bacon, two pounds rice, half-pound coffee, but I can't say beef, and you mustn't hope . . . but listen, this is a very rare exception, is that clear? You are a Sothron civilian, and we can't feed civilians, so you would do your fellow countrymen a favor if you asked them not to petition us, do you understand? Unless it is serious, I mean, *in extremis. (Pause.)* For God's sake, man, tell them not to beg like that, please!

MAN. I'd rather not, you know.

STRONG. I know, but please, tell them not to send those starving women to beg.

MAN. We'd rather not have to come, you know. Would you rather this back? *(Extends requisition form.)*

STRONG. *(Losing control.)* Get the hell out of here, and don't let me see you again.

MAN. We'd rather not have to come, you know. Thank ye. *(Exits.)*

HITCHCOCK. They pullin' your leg, a little, buster?

STRONG. Do you know Hitchcock, that there are people starving out there, literally starving, match-sticks, flat and bloated women, and these are white men, Hitchcock. How must it be out there?

HITCHCOCK. Winder-dressing. They gets a few of the corpsest bastards, scrofulitic and syphilitic and every other-itic, including no discernible pride, and they put them by the road just where you'll see them, especially.

STRONG. Who?

HITCHCOCK. Them. Sothroners. You gotta admire their clean and open dishonestness.

27

STRONG. They're starving, Hitchcock. I see signs of it every-where. Which means, I suggest, that there is a grave fault in our policy.

HITCHCOCK. Horseshit, buster. Horseshit. Them's gonna die will die. The rest is winder-dressing. A few dried-up bodies to make the Majors feel bad.

STRONG. (*Emphatically.*) That is simply not the way it is.

HITCHCOCK. Horseshit. And lemme tell you, buster, I wouldn't like to get caught handing food out to those mounteback sumbitches.

STRONG. It is an indisputable fact that there are people, a clear number that may even be the majority, who cannot find enough to support existence when we have taken what we needed and burned most of the rest of it. Now that is indisputable, and undeniable, and the command of this army will thank you to get your hair cut somewhere else.

HITCHCOCK. Horseshit! Winder-dressing, this command!

STRONG. I'm afraid I must insist.

HITCHCOCK. Insist alls you like, but you're just like us, Major, basically, iffen you can scrape through the dressing of horseshit. (*Laughs.*)

STRONG. Sgt. Dawson, remove Hitchcock.

HITCHCOCK. (*Wounded.*) Hey, man. Okay, okay.

STRONG. I'm telling you, Hitchcock, it is beyond contention that the effect of our policy is more than military: it is human as wide as the sea.

HITCHCOCK. (*With insolent warmth.*) Okay, Major.

MRS. ROBARTS. (*Entering.*) Was that man being sheared? Here? In the house?

STRONG. The lieutenant was just retiring, Mrs. Robarts. He knows what he has done is boorish.

HITCHCOCK. I got no finesse, Signora Robarts. And is there word from the Reverend?

STRONG. He managed a message since his capture, yes.

HITCHCOCK. An act of God, no damn doubt about it. With the major's permission. (*He exits, slowly, putting on shirt.*)

STRONG. (*To Mrs. Robarts.*) I apologize.

MRS. ROBARTS. You people all carry on so, you have such self-regard. (*Catching herself.*) I know, I know. I must be temperate. Would you assist me, Major, to the sofa. (*Two soldiers replace*

28

sofa into approximate same position it was in during Act One. Mrs. Robarts sits.) I want to see Sherman.

STRONG. He's not here.

MRS. ROBARTS. Well, is he gone, forever and ever?

STRONG. No.

MRS. ROBARTS. I thought he'd be gone forever and ever, at least. How can you subdue Georgia if you ensconce yourselves anywhere as long as a whole night?

STRONG. Well, there are military considerations.

MRS. ROBARTS. I daresay. Osterhaus on the left is almost a day behind the rest of you. It wouldn't do to isolate him back there, and leave all that flank unprotected?

STRONG. Have you been spying on us? Eavesdropping?

MRS. ROBARTS. No. (*Pause.*) Not militarily. We have been spying on your souls. We want to know what you have to say to each other and yourselves.

STRONG. You know, it will go bad for you if it is known that you have been spying for information about Osterhaus' lamentable pace, and . . . the rest of it. I'm sorry things have to be like that, but you ought not to play around with this military situation.

MRS. ROBARTS. I love to play. You're a bright man, Major, and well-spoken; don't be so God-awfully plain and stiff about everything.

STRONG. Well, this is serious.

MRS. ROBARTS. And who will cry you nay? I never said it wasn't deadly serious, as gloomy, cold, as damply serious as you can imagine in your New England heart. I just said it wasn't a military matter. (*Pause.*) Am I not right? You're a New Englander, a Bostonian perhaps?

STRONG. You defeat me.

MRS. ROBARTS. Mirabile dictu! I lived in Boston for several years with an Aunt who was finishing me. As you can see, I am resolutely finished. We are very much alike, Major Strong. And while we're on it, everyone knows Osterhaus is slow at everything and always has been. (*Pause.*) You remind me of my brother, also an alumnus of your law school at Harvard, though he was confined while there to the circle of hell reserved for Sothroners.

STRONG. Who?

MRS. ROBARTS. Never mind. He was killed six months ago. He

29

was likely the best man who ever lived, outside my father. (*Pause.*) Charles Colborne Law. Did you know him?

STRONG. He was very bright, well thought of, but strongly of the anti-abolitionist position. I'm sorry he's passed on.

MRS. ROBARTS. So am I. If I could have designed the way without damning him and damning me, I would have married him. Well, there's no future playing around with that one, is there?

STRONG. (*Laughing uncertainly.*) Oh, I think not.

MRS. ROBARTS. (*Suddenly determined, very charming.*) Now see here, Major Strong, you must tell me—we are so much alike you must tell me anything I want to know—tell me how I can bend Sherman to my will. I want only one thing, to free my husband. That, at least, is something I can do. And you must help me, we are so much alike.

STRONG. I can't do anything of the sort, you know that.

MRS. ROBARTS. I despair of what will happen when the North wins. We are counting on you, Major Strong, and all the Strongs and Steeles, they were your forebearers, am I not right? And a legion of decent people with some capacity. When the war is done, and you have won, and win you will, and win well, or very badly, and I don't mean you personally; when we are completely destroyed and gather ourselves together again to reconstruct this more perfect experiment we have been engaged in, we will need an underground of people in the North who are feelingly engaged with us: people of the classical stripe, passionate, rooted who lack all this unprincipaled ambition and cold method, method about everything, getting everything done, getting it all cleared up in time for dinner and amusements, that part of the day, methodical procreational activities. We shall need every well-placed man who knows that some people, some schemes, some ways of living are better, there is no other word for it, are better than any others, just as you know. It is really foolish to pretend you don't understand me, Major. Sherman, whom you worship, will gobble you up for lunch one day and explain the thing as necessity. I'm warning you.

STRONG. (*Hurt, bewildered, defensive.*) I don't worship the General. I admire his abilities.

MRS. ROBARTS. You love him like a father. Well, don't be ashamed of it. If I were in your place, I would love him, too, but

I would use my position, you can be sure: I would play him a little before me.

STRONG. It would be unbecoming for me to advance your cause.

MRS. ROBARTS. Is it unbecoming for people of the classical stripe to be heroic a little, as God means them to be?

STRONG. Your husband, Mrs. Robarts—I must tell you—may be the instrument by which the life of one or more of my comrades in arms will be saved from the savage, cowardly ambushes of your people, these passionate people who have lived by making other men slaves. Do you remember?

MRS. ROBARTS. That's Sherman talk, all that brazen swing of the scythe of what must be and canting explanation. I was speaking of love. What does it take to make you see love and hate, too, how you hate us, how you hate me, how you all do, every last one of you, blood-hate. And how you love us, too.

STRONG. What I feel is of no moment here.

MRS. ROBARTS. But it is. (*Pause.*) Well, Major, would you be so good as to bring me a glass of claret from that cabinet, and one for yourself? (*He does so.*) My life is nothing without objects which move me. I am moved now, dear Lord, I am exercised. (*They toast.*)

STRONG. (*Patiently.*) If, Mrs. Robarts, and I say if I ever have the General's attention sometime when he is disposed for things of a classical stripe, I will speak of Reverend Robarts, but I feel your husband is not important in all of this and you should know, simply as a matter of fact, you cannot approach Sherman. As a matter of fact, no one can approach him.

MRS. ROBARTS. (*Composed, smiling.*) Yet we are both alike. We must try. What is this short and now quite difficult life otherwise? (*Commotion from outside.*)

STRONG. Now if you would be so good as to go upstairs.

MRS. ROBARTS. (*Resolutly not moving.*) Ah, good, I see Sherman is coming.

STRONG. (*Firmly.*) You are a married woman, somewhat advanced in the term of her pregnancy. Remember that.

MRS. ROBARTS. I am not unfamiliar with any of my attributes, Major Strength.

STRONG. Strong.

MRS. ROBARTS. I meant Strong. Yes. (*Sherman enters, and is startled by seeing Mrs. Robarts, but goes on complacently.*)

SHERMAN. (*With unaccustomed harshness.*) Strong, will you see this is all put up again, except for my papers, and find that God-forsaken Hitchcock and have my horse ready. I mean at once, Strong.

STRONG. Yes, sir. (*He exits.*)

MRS. ROBARTS. Are you leaving now, General? Do you mean to travel at night?

SHERMAN. (*Curtly.*) How do you do, Mrs. Robarts? Are you feeling well?

MRS. ROBARTS. It is of no importance to me, your plans, but we are tired of our imprisonment.

SHERMAN. It won't be much longer.

MRS. ROBARTS. Glory Hallelujah! (*Mrs. Law enters, followed by Kate King. Mrs. Law seems frailer, more tired than previously. Her manner is belied by great exhaustion.*)

MRS. LAW. General Sherman. I demand to know of you, why two young men came to my rooms and took away the sword which belonged to my grandfather, which he carried against our common enemy, the British?

SHERMAN. Strong? Major Strong? Where the hell is Strong?

MRS. LAW. That was a monstrous breach of decorum, to take my old relic.

SHERMAN. (*Thundering.*) There is no decorum at this time, can't you understand that? (*Strong and Hitchcock enter.*) Strong, I thought I told you I wanted no women, no civilians of any kind in this room or near me.

STRONG. I know sir. They wouldn't stop her. They were afraid they'd have to injure her.

SHERMAN. Well, bloody hell, man bloody hell, then, injure her!

MRS. LAW. I want that sword returned.

SHERMAN. It is a weapon!

MRS. LAW. It is so badly rusted that had I the strength I could not withdraw it from the scabbard. Anything might be a weapon, the mood I'm in.

SHERMAN. Strong, find the bloody, Goddamn sword and give it back to Mrs. Law, if you would be so good.

MRS. LAW. (*Addressing the world.*) He is insolent beyond the compass of his high office, this God! (*She is seized with pain and collapses. The women catch her, Strong fetches a chair, and they sit her down.*)

32

MRS. ROBARTS. Mother!

SHERMAN. (*To Hitchcock.*) Get Sherborne. (*To women.*) Major Sherborne is the finest surgeon we have and he will attend to her. I am truly sorry her endurance has been so taxed. (*To Strong.*) Strong, I will not stay here. Have my papers brought to division headquarters. Bring everything. I will not stay here.

STRONG. Yes sir.

MRS. ROBARTS. General Sherman, please!

SHERMAN. I am not staying here.

MRS. ROBARTS. (*Helplessly.*) Would you please release my husband? He meant no harm to anyone and will do no harm once he is free. He is a man of God.

SHERMAN. I make it my rule never to interfere with subordinates in administrative details. I'm sure the matter will straighten itself.

MRS. ROBARTS. I am begging you General, please. (*Falls to her knees.*) I am begging you.

SHERMAN. Do not beg.

MRS. ROBARTS. You cannot stop me.

SHERMAN. No, but I need not listen. (*Starts to go.*)

MRS. ROBARTS. You will kill me. At the very least, you will kill my child.

SHERMAN. No. You will kill him. Jeff Davis will kill him, if anyone. South Carolina will kill him. I have nothing to do with it. My hands are clean.

MRS. ROBARTS. (*Going into a hysterical fit.*) Jesu Savior!

SHERMAN. Holmes? McCready? Where in bloody hell is someone who can do something? (*To Mrs. Robarts.*) I know this is calculated, Mrs. Robarts. (*Her fit continues, to Kate.*) Do something!

KATE. I don't know what to do.

SHERMAN. I know this is calculated, Mrs. Robarts. (*Goes to where she is writhing.*) I will have your husband shot, do you hear what the bloody hell I'm saying? I will have him drawn and quartered. (*Impotently.*) Now stop. (*Bends down, and brings her up, holding her.*) Now stop! (*Less angry, more tenderly.*) Now stop! (*She continues to heave.*) Now stop! (*She begins to relax.*) Now stop! Please (*Her head falls back, exhausted.*) Please.

MRS. ROBARTS. (*Broken.*) Yes.

SHERMAN. (*Easing her into his rocker.*) Sit here. (*Strong enters*

33

with Sutler. Kate, Jussie and Sutler help Mrs. Law to her feet, and upstairs. Strong remains.)

STRONG. *(To Kate.)* If you will help Mrs. Law to her room, Major Sherborne will be there in a moment. *(To General.)* General, your horse is ready, sir. That God-forsaken Hitchcock fellow got it ready for you. You know, he's not so bad after all, General?

SHERMAN. Good for you Strong. Go along with it, for a moment.

STRONG. General, I think we should withdraw now. I think we should leave these people.

SHERMAN. Thank you, Major. Would you be so good as to pour a whiskey for myself and then get out of here, you and everybody else?

STRONG. *(Boldly.)* What we should do, General, is that we should not— *(Intimately.)* Uncle Billy?

SHERMAN. I appreciate your concern, son, I do. Please don't bite my back, son.   . .

STRONG. Yes sir *(Pours a whiskey, and exits.)*

SHERMAN. *(After a moment.)* I have seldom been so ill-used, Mrs. Robarts, seldom so humiliated.

MRS. ROBARTS. *(Regaining herself.)* That is not true.

SHERMAN. Well, you mean what they wrote in the newspaper that I was insane, Cump Sherman raving, you mean that?

MRS. ROBARTS. No.

SHERMAN. I wasn't insane. I was right. But there were pressures, and I was correct to resign my commission—it was the proper thing to do—and I suppose that had it not been for my children, I would have taken my own life violently.

MRS. ROBARTS. *(Wearily.)* I didn't mean that.

SHERMAN. I'll tell you what it was. There were newspapermen around, rabble, opportunists, the worst sort of men. I wouldn't come to them in the least and they paid me back, the way they pay back politicians and lawyers and the fashionable military leaders, the men who must pay these dogs and all the dogs some bucket of vomit to measure their own dignities. I was in great pain, in consequence of not being believed. They simply would not believe that the total Confederate force was over thirty thousand and I myself needed an additional ten thousand men, and the Secretary of War could not see—well, how could he, on a visit of two days, three days—could not see that our condition was perilous. No, it was worse than that; it was like the shadow of death itself. He could not see honestly how many were out there, just precisely how many of them, and, so, I was humiliated and resigned. I suppose when they all write their memoirs of this conflict, the men who were on the other side—and I know them, most of them, they were my classmates—when they tell us how many of them were out there, waiting, then my fears will not seem to have been so rootless. I will be in eternity, with my name, my wife, my dear children, but perhaps I will be saved some of the anguish, if that matters, which I was not saved here, on this earth, alone. I treated those rotten dogs, of the rotten, popular rabble press badly because, you see, I was afraid within, a great sharp active pain which pierced me and which I could not stop, and because I could not stop that pain I would have hung them all or taken their presses and melted them molten hot and poured the mess into their bowels, yes, no bloody outrage would have been enough to satisfy me. (*Pause.*) But I wasn't mad, so you mustn't think that of me. I was saddened often because I was not believed in the military, which is my life, and because any life that I have tried beyond the military has been chaos, because my banks have failed—they cannot be mastered— even tranquility failed because I could not master a mob in California and was made a joke of for trying: these ruined banks, these failed positions I have tried outside the military, which is my life, the chaos which set in everywhere, the dogs themselves redeemed by it, by this mob rule, which is killing us: I could not master it. (*Pause.*) It was Bull Run, that set the cap on it. You have never seen human bodies, the bodies of men, so badly defiled, all that flesh filled with capacities, and it became swill, raw swill, in every shape, mangled, and the horses without mounts ran on, blood flowing from their nostrils, except the ones that were hitched to the shattered caissons, and they lay on the ground, gnawing at their sides. "Thou are beautiful, o my love, comely as Jerusalem, terrible as an army with banners." The Song of Solomon. "Stay me with flagons, comfort me with apples, for I am sick of love." Or the conflict, or I was then. Grant's right to be a sot when he has to; I never could. (*Pause.*) Yes, I have been melancholic, but that is a thing of the past. Now I have found my station. I never was really insane.

MRS. ROBARTS. I didn't think so.

SHERMAN. Perhaps you didn't.

MRS. ROBARTS. I meant you have been ill-used before, if not by me, then by others. I believe you have been kept down, Sherman, and so have I.

SHERMAN. I have not always tried so strenuously at anything as I have at soldiering.

MRS. ROBARTS. Why not?

SHERMAN. It has not always been fitting.

MRS. ROBARTS. No?

SHERMAN. I have been hesitant, at times, like yourself, circumspect.

MRS. ROBARTS. I am not a General.

SHERMAN. Well, I am just a lucky man whose skills happened to meet the exigencies of a moment I had rather not existed.

MRS. ROBARTS. You persist in your fib. You love this! It is a dog's dinner to you. (*Pause.*) What were you afraid of?

SHERMAN. I don't know, would you believe that? But I think when I was most troubled, I was alone, and that was the pain of it. I was alone as no man has ever been since Cain when he heard it was quiet, after his brother ceased breathing, the bone in his hand. Utterly bereft, you might say, cut off forever.

MRS. ROBARTS. I knew.

SHERMAN. How did you know?

MRS. ROBARTS. I didn't. I wanted to say something to suggest that I might be intimate with your thoughts. Fancy that!

SHERMAN. (*Exasperated.*) Then am I to be held up in this matter of your husband?

MRS. ROBARTS. Held up? Ill-used? Sherman, you amaze me in this posture of love, or whatever you might call it. You talk as though someone had trapped you, and you were the unlucky legatee of this long, terrible evening's sport.

SHERMAN. I cannot escape the inference that I will be taken advantage of if I succumb to any of your quiet, quite moving beauty, Mrs. Robarts. I have always been open to such tender beauty, the beauty of your land here, these comfortable establishments. I've lived here, you know that. I remember how I was made to feel I wanted so much from you, how easy it was to desire certain things and then forget one's self and not be as careful as one ought to be. You Sothroners have always drawn me out, but I've shown you something: I'm not such an easy mark.

MRS. ROBARTS. I was feeling sorry for you tonight, for the first time, you bloody Sherman. I think you were asking for my pity and such mean little ways as I could muster for your comfort. And I concluded I must do something for your sake and for my own, but I don't know what. What can I do for you, you bloody Sherman, that will matter? Will you take my prayers, and my sorrow?

SHERMAN. I must warn you that I cannot and will not interfere with subordinates in this matter of your husband and I must say that I feel aggrieved that it should be between us, or between any people, like that sharp point of pain. That's hard and I'm sorry, but I do not like to be beholding, which is what you attempt to make me.

MRS. ROBARTS. I was wishing to hope to want to love you with compassionate passion, you bloody man. Is that so hard?

SHERMAN? Why?

MRS. ROBARTS. I have no idea in the world. I am raw with fretting and it's a deal since I sat down to a decent table. I am angry, too. So there! This way is as good as any.

SHERMAN. You are obtuse, Mrs. Robarts. If not your husband, than what, as you are, is it that you want from me?

MRS. ROBARTS. (*Defeated.*) I don't know. If you would set my husband free, that would do for now, that would suffice.

SHERMAN. I don't know. I don't think so. (*Pause.*) Well, I know what I want. (*With great effort.*) I want to put my hand on your head, to touch your hair. Would that be acceptable?

MRS. ROBARTS. (*Frustrated.*) That would be acceptable. (*Sherman crosses, and puts his hand on her head. At first, it is a grave, monumental act, then his hand begins to move on her head, slowly, feeling the texture of her hair, and interlaces his fingers with her hair. He has averted his eyes, and Mrs. Robarts, who has been still through this, now extends her hand, and they lock fingers. Mrs. Robarts suddenly jumps up, moves away, and then towards him, and kisses him. They mutually embrace. Sherman's hands slide down her body. Then, suddenly, Mrs. Robarts pulls away.*) Oh, no, Uncle Billy, I think not, not now, not at this moment. (*Sherman stands, looking at her, awkwardly.*) I must go upstairs, do you understand me?

SHERMAN. I will follow you, if that would not too heavily indebt us; do you understand *me?*

MRS. ROBARTS. I wish you would come along, certainly. (*She goes to doors, opens them, steps into hall, and turns to look at him*

37

once more. She then continues upstairs. He crosses to desk, but just as he gets there, he stops suddenly.)

SHERMAN. *(Self-pleased.)* Great God in heaven, I am ACCEPT-ABLE! *(He follows her. The soldiers, who have been standing guard outside, exit, and Kate King enters through the portico windows into the room.)*

KATE. *(Calling after her.)* Well come ahead. *(Sutler enters.)* There's no one left. There's no one anywhere.

SUTLER. Gone, but not forgotten, I surmise.

KATE. Now.

SUTLER. Now what?

KATE. The next thing.

SUTLER. What next thing?

KATE. The next thing I don't know about. What's going to happen to me?

SUTLER. It is, or will be, along the lines where your imagination has already directed you.

KATE. *(Emphatic.)* But I don't know. I don't imagine that!

SUTLER. How sweet! *(Makes to embrace her.)*

KATE. No, I want to know exactly what's going to happen!

SUTLER. It will not be unpleasant.

KATE. Well, let me tell you, that I have heard a thing or two concerning this and that and your generous assurances are not at all assuring.

SUTLER. It will not hurt. Well, yes, perhaps it will, a little at first. I have no first-hand knowledge of these things and I must say I don't care. Sometimes, I'm told, it is absolutely nothing. Sometimes, it takes away the whole taste, so I'm told. These things have been borne, Katharine, so many thousands have borne them before. I am a careful and tender trader, Katharine, and I can regulate your pain to benefit. I am interested that you experience some degree of pleasure yourself, as is befitting. I will not steal you blind!

KATE. I should hope not!

SUTLER. Take my hand, come with me, and I will take you, wherever.

KATE. I thought I would have to be drunk first on some heady old, hoary old bottle of something or other. Can it be right just to accept you like this?

SUTLER. My dear Katharine, don't talk so bloody much.

38

KATE. But I do, I love to know things, everything. (*They make to embrace, but are interrupted by a knock on the door.*)

STRONG. (*Offstage.*) General Sherman?

SUTLER. Oh for the love of . . . the Union! (*Sutler takes Kate by the hand, and they go off.*)

STRONG. (*He enters room.*) General? (*Pause.*) General Sherman? (*Angry.*) William Tecumseh Sherman! What the hell! (*Throws papers on desk.*) Well, fuck it. Fuck him. (*Takes book from coat pocket, sits in General's rocker.*)

HITCHCOCK. (*Entering like a thief.*) Major Strong!

STRONG. Hello Hitchcock.

HITCHCOCK. Henry.

STRONG. (*Grudgingly, affectionately.*) 'Lo, Henry. Damn it all man.

HITCHCOCK. Regular fuggeroo-buggeroo of a day, and a night and a war, eh, Major?

STRONG. It's this business, Henry, the whole transaction, this bloody conflict. It's not the least what I was taught to feel. All we do is take things, every bloody thing we can get our hands on.

HITCHCOCK. You been drinkin'?

STRONG. A little.

HITCHCOCK. Well, who done what to you?

STRONG. Nobody.

HITCHCOCK. Well, bullshit, then.

STRONG. I want to be a regular soldier, Henry, and be honestly scared in my pants and not be back here, watching everything.

HITCHCOCK. I don't think so, Major. That's all sweet shit, so much noise. There's gonna be time for all that brave sweet shit and articles and recommendations and commendations and accommodations and commentaries, that squeezing it out—that'll be later on when the whole mess is swallowed like a lump of spit. This here's the damndest thing Major, ain't that right? (*Puts his hand on Strong's shoulder.*)

STRONG. I don't give a good Goddamn.

HITCHCOCK. (*Pulls his hand back.*) Well, fuck you Major.

STRONG. Hey, lieutenant, I'm greatly sorry, and much obliged. I do not wish to be alone.

HITCHCOCK. Well, it's not a kind thing, even I appreciate that. My stupid brother got kilt, my oldest friend, kilt. My daddy was shot in the foot, so he'll never be no good. You just don't know.

39

My old friend there was the worst coward, Major, and one night when we were gonna bed down, he made me sleep on the side nearest the enemy so's I'd be the one to stop any shot. And I said to him, You're crazy, and he said, mebbe, but I intend to survive, because life is everything and there's nothing else. He was kilt that very night, lying next to me, by a ball some damn fool fired in the air near us. Damn thing went up and came down and went right through his eye to his brains. He wasn't more 'n two feet off. (*Pause.*) They're gonna shoot that reverend who's husband of the crazy woman.

STRONG. They won't.

HITCHCOCK. I heard. He's accused a spy.

STRONG. In the name of God, who set this up? Sherman? Did Sherman order the execution?

HITCHCOCK. Nobody ordered it. It's by the book.

STRONG. I have never been so sorry. The General must be told.

HITCHCOCK. (*Pause.*) Hey, Major, I wanna lie straight by you, tonight. I'm gonna show you something, I am.

STRONG. (*Surprised, touched.*) Why do you want to?

HITCHCOCK. I'm horny, man, hell is just as bright as that. I want some ease.

STRONG. Well, so do I, so do I. But I've got to extricate myself from this God-awful obligation to care so much about these people: the woman, all the women, Sherman, even you, Henry.

HITCHCOCK. Well, I'm sure it's a serious problem but there's not a hell of a lot to do about it now, so come on, Major, or we'll be the only heroes awake tonight, outside the pickets, and I wouldn't put no money out there, hell, no. Now come on, Major. It's okay. Everything's okay. (*They exit. Lights fade.*)

ACT III

Dawn. Sutler is fully dressed, and curled on the floor. Kate is sitting next to him, singing softly. She hears the door open, and quickly lies down, pulling her shawl over her. Mrs. Law enters, and crosses to Sherman's desk.

MRS. LAW. Humph. (*Hearing Sutler, she opens blind.*) Very well, now I have accounted for everyone. There is good Kate King, sleeping next to a man. How will she ever stay good in this conflict? And when Mary, my good daughter, when Mary would sit up half the night disputing with a Federal officer and in her own darkened rooms. She cannot remain blameless either. (*She picks up pitcher from desk.*) There's for you, King Commerce! (*She pours water on Sutler.*) Be a man, be so good as a man, and leave this poor girl in peace. Good morning. (*She exits. Kate begins to laugh at the damp Sutler.*)

SUTLER. Well, I am damned!

KATE. Most likely.

SUTLER. And how long have you been waiting, and watching, Katharine King? Well?

    A dollar shalt thou have, and present pay—
    And liquor likewise will I give to thee
    And friendship shall combine and brotherhood:
    Is this not just?— For I shall Sutler be
    Unto the camp, and profits will accrue.
    Give me thy hand.

KATE. I shall have my dollar?

SUTLER. In cash, most justly paid.

KATE. Well, then, that's the humor of it. (*Sutler drops her hand, she stops quoting.*) Except I mean to follow you, Sutler, wherever you go.

SUTLER. Can't be done.

→ KATE. Well, I mean to. What if it is impossible, I can do it. You love me.

SUTLER. Listen to me. When the war is over, and it will be within twelve months, I will come back for you my dear . . .

41

Katherine, and find you wherever you are, and spirit you away to a new life.

KATE. No, I will be properly married by then. Now is my only chance for something better.

SUTLER. Don't get married. Wait for me, my poor chicken.

KATE. I won't wait for you or any man. I'm not that sort. I have to get along quickly. What would you have me do for a year— dear God! A whole year!— Read novels? Study childbearing and nurture? Listen to the horsemen go by in the evening? I want to do something I could not heretofore have imagined myself doing: like loving you, sir, alone and personally; loving you and being with you is my destiny.

SUTLER. You cannot, Katharine. You would have, first, no place to come home to, your own good people having read you out of their hearts. And you would have no place to go elsewhere, myself being an adventurer and unlikely for a while to take root. You would be between and between ceaselessly.

KATE. But in your company, my dear doctor, that's what matters, in your capable hands. Among your very capable arms.

SUTLER. They all feel like you do, in the first flush. It's like taking too much wine too fast. Whoosh!

KATE. You don't take me seriously when nonetheless I am being serious and strong to such a pitch that I will follow and dog and haunt you everywhere and cry out by the tents at night so that shame alone will compel you to recognize me and that I love you and you will be forced to ask me to come in at last to your tent.

SUTLER. Why won't you listen to sense, since you are educated proper and straight? This is your home.

KATE. I have no taste for it.

SUTLER. It is not a matter of taste. Just wait for me and we will do what is expected of us, which will eventually please all the generations.

KATE. I don't believe you love me. You are not passionate.

SUTLER. (*Passionately.*) I am, I am! But I have to plan. What if this is nothing? We will find out. Oh, would I *could* have you this moment in the due course of things! There, that is a passionate sentence, as passionate as I get: I am after being in love with you.

KATE. Again.

SUTLER. I am after . . . (*They embrace.*) I love you. You've pulled it out of me; it was stuck.

KATE. Again.

SUTLER. I love you.

KATE. Make love to me again. There, I said it. I asked for it. How do you like that?

SUTLER. Oh, you are a preposterous little thing, a perfect silly girl, (*Pause.*) but for whom I am after feeling strongly.

KATE. I am plainly confused. Why can't I have what I want when I have it? I mean, why can't I keep it?

SUTLER. Oh, if you could, in tender mercy, answer that question you would have attained the position of an eminent learned person and they would follow you, believe me, all those dissatisfied people, those men and women who in payment for their lack of what they want that they had and cannot have—their loves, agility, a talent, fortune, anything—flock to me and my progeny, to buy things. And they always have, war and peace, come to buy. Some day a great-granddaughter of mine will ask her mother what it was that Samuel Sutler was that he achieved such eminence and wealth, and the mother—my granddaughter—will say: he was a merchant, dear child, he sold objects to people for money: bottled attars of ardor and amour, booze, rags, gleaming pins which arrested the eye, fruits and candy, salts, and meat, exotic textures and rough, plain grains and milled flour, gew-gaws and gaudy bows and ties, manuals on conception and elimination, licorice, luxury, liquorishness: sold all these, for cash, to disappointed and hungry people who at one time had something they wanted and did not see why they couldn't keep, but keep it they couldn't, so they had to be spending and your great-grandfather provided them with all they sought, for a generation at least and he has been dead fifty years now and they are still waiting to buy his stuff. (*Pause.*) That's me, dead fifty years! What a legacy. (*Pause.*) Most people just get on with it, you know, and get some meaningful thing. Take Sherman. One son of his, a lad of about nine or ten soldiering all the hell over one of Sherman's fine military camps, a son he showed off to the delectation of all beholders, and plainly, one he loved too much, contracted typhoid fever from being shown off and delected and died and was sent back to Saint Louis in a lead box, a hole in his father's heart. What does he stuff into the void? The bloody Sothron body, which he bought with blood. Sherman is the single man I have ever known with such a passion for his bereavement. Nothing like me. I am capable of loving you, even when I have what I want and can't have it. (*Suddenly, agitated.*) But why not, in the name of God?

KATE. (*Excited.*) Yes, why not? Take me with you. I bow before you, doctor, and I raise you up.

SUTLER. Let me think. Go someplace so I can be here and think what it is like to want you when I've lost all the shiny new-mint brightness of your immediate self. Let me test what it will be to miss you.

KATE. Well, that's very fine, I will. But don't steal off now, the way men have done, time out of mind.

SUTLER. I won't I promise. (*She exits.*) I think I promise. I have a powerful urge to steal off. Can you imagine that?

STRONG. (*Entering, his old crisp self.*) Sutler, good day.

SUTLER. Strong.

STRONG. Have you seen General Sherman?

SUTLER. Rarely so well.

STRONG. Today, I mean, this morning.

SUTLER. I know what you mean, linthead. He's stirring someplace.

STRONG. He's vanished.

SUTLER. Poof!

STRONG. Look, if he had been needed, what would I have done?

SUTLER. Knocked on the door.

STRONG. I see.

SUTLER. It's his entitlement. This is war, boy; war is war and you can make nothing else of it; Sherman said that. War's a mixed blessing; I said that. Speaking of entitlement, where would you have been last night, had the cause needed you?

STRONG. I was nearby.

SUTLER. Well, so were we all, and similiarly engaged. What would they say of us in the midst of all this killing if we took no time for kindness, or what passes for kindness amongst us?

STRONG. Don't be so hard, Sutler, I don't like it.

SUTLER. I am a lamb, Strong, I assure you. You are the most enlisted man I ever met in this fray.

STRONG. Why do you say that? I don't like that either.

SUTLER. You are the most conscripted. But tain't so, son: that's not really blood on your hands now, is it?

STRONG. I don't know what it is. Dried something.

SUTLER. Dried seed. (*Pause.*) Now be easier on the rest of us, Major, and we'll see someday you are honorably discharged.

STRONG. I must be blunt to say that I don't like you, Sutler, and I resent it that you have the General's ear.

SUTLER. So what? What am I going to do with the General's ear? Sell it? You have his heart, you and this whore of a territory. And all of that to some degree surprises me, because I thought him quite unsentimental.

STRONG. I am bound to repeat, I don't approve of you or your tone.

SUTLER. You've said it, now go away and wash your hands!

STRONG. (*A sudden burst.*) Goddamn it! (*Recovering.*) I beg your pardon.

SUTLER. Begged, delivered, accepted, I trust. Blow on. Would you mind if I left?

STRONG. (*Badly sarcastic.*) Not much, Doctor.

SUTLER. Well if you knew why it was that I seemed hard to you, Major, then you would know why it is, Major, in general, that you are an insufferable little prick. (*He exits.*)

HITCHCOCK. (*Enters through window, he has been eavesdropping.*) Well, Robert—

STRONG. Major.

HITCHCOCK. Yes, sir, Major. Best pack it up. He's got his point, the drummer. We ain't been the best of soldiers since we begun this little foray through Georgia, no sir, we all been a little loose.

STRONG. Exactly, Henry.

HITCHCOCK. Lieutenant.

STRONG. Lieutenant.

HITCHCOCK. We been crazy, and killin', and concupiscent and he knows it, the drummer, and I know it, and you sure as hell know it, and fifty thousand men, they know it, and the General, he first of all knows it and he knows we all know it, fifty thousand strong, but, you know, Major, the General doesn't even want to know he knows it, let alone we know it neither: shit, we better wake up every morning, virginal, you just ask Uncle Bill. (*Pause.*) This here's a real virginal morning, ain't it?

STRONG. It's another day, Lieutenant.

HITCHCOCK. Yeah, I can see that. I suppose back in Boston you're very highly regarded, Major: they probably have high hopes for you. But still I don't think you know piss-all about life.

STRONG. What life? This one? This bloody one? The next?

HITCHCOCK. The last one, Major, the last horseshitting one, yesterday. (*As Hitchcock replaces General's glass of whiskey, Sherman enters. Hitchcock starts out of room, and stands at attention by the General. He motions for him to leave. Sherman goes to his desk, and Strong goes to leave, but is stopped by Sherman.*)

SHERMAN. Strong, at your convenience, would you pass the word to Osterhaus that General Sherman would be greatly pleased if he, Osterhaus, did not butcher that bloody God-bothering Reverend Robarts but instead returned the same undeserving God-bothering Reverend bastard to his natural bed and board. Would you do that?

STRONG. They're going to shoot him today.

SHERMAN. Really? Then would you do that immediately. Would you tell Osterhaus that it would please me to have this done, it would ease my own predicament, but that I am not ordering him and if the prayerful Reverend is fated ineluctably to be extirpated, then that is how it must be. Only that it is my pleasure he not be, nothing more?

STRONG. Yes sir. (*Exits. Jussie enters with coffee tray, places it on Sherman's desk, leaves as courier enters with papers. Mrs. Robarts also enters. Sherman dismisses the courier.*)

MRS. ROBARTS. Good morning.

SHERMAN. We agreed, I thought, that you were to stay up there in those agreeable rooms till we were gone.

MRS. ROBARTS. This is my house. Your request I deemed unreasonable. Besides, I want to look at you. You are the most American specimen I ever saw: so tall and lanky, with that thatched hair that looks hacked with a hatchet that you are forever worrying with your hands. The demented gaze occasionally in your eyes, bizarre in the civilized world, but American, exactly and properly.

SHERMAN. I had thought we'd parted company amiably, cordially. I had thought we got on rather well.

MRS. ROBARTS. We did.

SHERMAN. Then why is it that you are railing at me?

MRS. ROBARTS. I am not railing. I am commenting. I was paying you a compliment by making you an apotheosis and in the next breath I was going to tell you that, contrary to good sense, I approved of this American warrior, virtue's thief.

46

SHERMAN. You are the worst harpie in the world, really.

MRS. ROBARTS. I am not.

SHERMAN. Well, be reverential a little, be tender. It is more becoming in a woman.

MRS. ROBARTS. I expect you to be with us when the war is over. I expect your active support. They will make you or that tosspot Grant president of the land, be sure of it. We expect to be remembered, our debts are paid.

SHERMAN. I am in the military where I belong; stop trying to puff me up. You must suffer what you suffer for acts of treason and anarchy. There's an end to it. Now, let us not discuss political matters on any account. (*Pause.*) And you must stop tying to conscript every man-jack of us to your wild cause.

MRS. ROBARTS. Major Strong, you mean?

SHERMAN. Yes, and Olson, that subaltern Burns, a bright boy, but innocent. This is the military; some other General would have your tongue cut out.

MRS. ROBARTS. For what?

SHERMAN. Treason and anarchy. Pride. Don't force me to be a pig about this. I am in personal debt to you for a kindness, and admire you, in fact.

MRS. ROBARTS. You speak as though in pain. It is a good thing we did not fall fast in love, Sherman, the earth would crack with your saying it. My husband—

SHERMAN. They wanted to shoot the pious bastard. I surmise he is, at least, pious, but they won't shoot him as a favor to me.

MRS. ROBARTS. I was going to say my husband would disapprove of our intimacy.

SHERMAN. Then don't tell him.

MRS. ROBARTS. I will have to.

SHERMAN. That is you business. I never expect to hear from you again. I would not be happy if I ever had word from you.

MRS. ROBARTS. Ashamed, Sherman?

SHERMAN. No, no, I don't think so. I have been ashamed of slovenliness, at times, and at times, of willfulness, of retreat or retrenching where I oughtn't, of a few slight excesses. I have been, I told you, ashamed once of myself overall, had trouble breathing, considered my end near. There is much to regret, Mrs. Robarts, but not my knowing you. We were fairly served; we matched well.

MRS. ROBARTS. Well, may we leave it then that I traded myself for my husband's life. All that makes more sense to me, and you have a peddler's sense of propriety after all. Really! I have to be paid with something, since this is harlotry, but I don't care about that. I must have something from you, your good estimation, an after-thought. You must give me more than a poke; you must think well of me.

SHERMAN. You have my good estimation.

MRS. ROBARTS. Oh? (*Cooly.*) I am inclined to believe that when this is over and you are done stringing us up, in a few months, I will end up very coarse. I will be a terrible, hard bitch, unconquerable.

SHERMAN. Good for you, then, because I am a notorious son of that same hard species. We'll grind it all up, you and I, and it has been, may I say, momentous.

MRS. ROBARTS. It has been exciting and rotten and I feel quite empty. (*Disentangling herself after a brief embrace.*) Well, you've got to march, Sherman, so march, and I don't wish you well, I really don't: I had to try to cut you down a little. It took up the night at least.

SHERMAN. Quite so. (*Pause.*) They're coming now. It would be better all around if you went to your rooms. I dislike to say goodbye and goodbye again.

MRS. ROBARTS. (*With firm love.*) Very well. Goodbye. (*Pause.*) And goodbye again. (*As she exits to portico,* Strong and soldiers *appear.*)

STRONG. General, these things arrived when you were gone, sir, when you couldn't be reached.

SHERMAN. "Things" Strong? That's not very precise. Papers, man, dispatches, we say in the military. Is there anything important?

STRONG. I don't know. Should I have opened these papers, sir, these dispatches, as we say in the military, in the General's absence, and read them and attempted to interpret them and then sounded a general alarm for the General to acquaint him with my interpretations of these papers, sir, these dispatches, as we say in the military?

SHERMAN. (*White-hot anger.*) Don't say anymore, Strong, not now and not ever in the future. You are not competent to take the position you take and to muster the insolence with which you advance your position. Remember your function and perform it so well, so perfectly, that I will never have any occasion to find fault with you. We have no contact beyond one of rank, you must be absolutely beholden. Otherwise, you can go to hell! Do you understand?

STRONG. I do not, I believe, do not, I think I can say, truthfully, understand and this is, as a matter of fact, a species of hell, so your wishing me otherwise to go where I already am is not a threat, sir. I have concluded that we—this army—are irrevocably in the wrong, morally and God-foreknowingly in the wrong in how we have conducted this malignant rooting-out and rooting-up of this land and these people. And I must forbid myself from having any further part of it, and you sir, you must forbid yourself from having any further part of it.

SHERMAN. I AM IT! ALL OF IT! Wipe your eyes, you hopeless son of a bitch; they're wet as a woman's. Hitchcock!

HITCHCOCK. Sir!

SHERMAN. Major Robert Steele Strong has been relieved of his his duties and is now under arrest for insubordination and conduct unbecoming an officer and a gentleman. Would you see that this information is recorded and that the Major is held in accordance to his rank?

HITCHCOCK. Yes sir.

SHERMAN. Now get out of here.

STRONG. Yes sir. (*He takes off sword and extends it to Sherman.*)

SHERMAN. Hitchcock! (*Indicating that Hitchcock should take the sword, which he does. Strong salutes, exits.*)

MRS. ROBARTS.

    Butcher, barker, army chief,

    Banker, lawyer, Strong's defeat.

SUTLER. Well, now. Can you fancy this, General?

SHERMAN. Napoleon brandy?

SUTLER. Buried in the orchard, but there's not much you can do about that now. Them good old bummers found the buried gold last night and I reckon every drop's been converted to sweat and piss by now, except for this bottle, for which I paid dearly. Would you join me in earnest to your continued success?

MRS. ROBARTS. That bottle is ours, sir, ours!

SUTLER. I bought it from a man who had possession, a crucial nine-tenths of the relevant law on the matter.

MRS. ROBARTS. You, sir, are a son of a bitch, and so are you all, all sons of bitches.

KATE. Mary Robarts, he is not, he is not, you're not fair!

MRS. ROBARTS. Be quiet, Kate King! You're little better than a whore yourself.

SUTLER. And you are Mary Magdalene? (*Sherman looks hard at Sutler.*)

MRS. ROBARTS. Shut-up, you vulturing son-of-a-bitch.

MRS. LAW. Dear! This concatenation nearly subdues me. General Sherman, I asked to be allowed to come within the circle of your presence so that I might personally thank you for returning that poor ancestral relic, the sword that was taken last night. You were very God-like, General, in your mercy to have it restored to me.

MRS. ROBARTS. (*Coldly.*) Yes, thank you.

SHERMAN. Sutler, would you give that bottle to the colored woman to be put by for the family?

SUTLER. I will not. I am a civilian.

SHERMAN. (*White hot.*) Give her the goddamn bottle. We are not thieves! (*Sutler does so, wordlessly.*) Good day. I am in your debt, ladies.

HITCHCOCK. 'Hut.

SHERMAN. That is all there is.

HITCHCOCK. Ho. (*Soldiers move out.*)

SUTLER. (*To Kate.*)

> Look to thy chattels and thy moveables;
> Let senses rule; the word is pitch and pay.
> Trust none,
> For oaths are straws, men's faiths are wafer cakes,
> And hold fast is the only dog, my duck. (*Pause.*)
> Next year, Kate. Be constant (*He exits.*)

KATE. (*Frantic.*) NOOOO!!!!!

MRS. ROBARTS. (*Stopping Kate.*) You will spoil yourself no further.

KATE. You have no right. I love him. I love him.

MRS. ROBARTS. You don't love him. It's all a base little itchiness. Now stay still. (*The women stand frozen, listening. For the first time since the start, it is absolutely silent.*) They may come or they may come, but . . .

KATE. What?

MRS. LAW. We will hew to our business.

50

MRS. ROBARTS. It appears that I shall have to stay in Georgia. Where could I go? North? I will never live there: that would be farcical. England? There is simply no magnitude in England; Europe, all the rest of the world but here is too small. There is no danger. Well, what am I saying? I can't stay, I can't go? You'll be laughing in a minute.

MRS. LAW. I am certain that I shall stay, that I shall be buried here soon. I have been troubling God and your father so unconscionably of late, owning up to my miserable frailities; I am always owning up to these miserable frailities: but my dear children, it turns out—and this surprises me—that I was better before, when young, than now, when I am nothing but snappish and dry. I'll be gone when your child is born, make of it what you will.

MRS. ROBARTS. I make of it that you will live much longer, Mother. It is in our family.

KATE. I'm going, Mary Robarts, what is there to stay for? One of these coming summers you will find me in Europe, at the finest hotel, sipping mineral water in the late afternoon, when it is most pleasant. My rich husband will be rich, my beautiful children will be perfect, and I will have many lovers, of different sorts. I feel absolutely positive this is going to happen when everything is settled here. (*Pause.*) Don't you think so?

MRS. ROBARTS. No.

KATE. I think that is too, too awfully dark, too awful. Don't say anymore, Mary Robarts.

MRS. ROBARTS. I won't. (*The three soldiers, this time with smoldering torches enter onto the portico.*)

KATE. More soldiers.

MRS. LAW. Now Kate, what's left?

MRS. ROBARTS. Nothing, Mama, nothing. We will not concern ourselves. (*Soldiers enter with smoldering torches.*)

KATE. O, dear heavens!

MRS. LAW. It is the house.

MRS. ROBARTS. (*With grim acceptance.*) It is nothing.

SOLDIER ONE. Morning.

KATE. (*Desperate.*) Did you come for the brandy? We found we do have a bottle after all.

MRS. ROBARTS. No.

MRS. LAW. Mary, I don't believe we were meant to keep it.

SOLDIER ONE. Tain't the brandy, no ma'am.

MRS. ROBARTS. Is it my husband?

SOLDIER ONE. Well, when they came to point their muskets at him, the Reverend, he wet his pants: who wouldn't but he didn't pewl none, the way some scream out about such and so. He spoke, sort of, in that voice of his, he says, his boys, they were like children year before last, their faces soft as a woman's and now they've been like men—and us, the bluebacks, we was something else, we never were like children nor women nor nothing else, we didn't have mothers, no we were the engines from hell, wonderful to watch, he says, magnificent to behold. His last speech, (*Pause.*) before they let him go. With the General's compliments, he leaves you three horses, a spavin' mule and the Reverend, who's coming home upon it.

KATE. Well, that is exceptional news.

MRS. LAW. Isn't it?

MRS. ROBARTS. Yes.

SOLDIER ONE. Best of this day to you. (*They exit.*)

KATE. I think what they really wanted was the brandy.

MRS. LAW. It was the house.

MRS. ROBARTS. Then they should have set the torch to it. We have still to taste our defeat.

MRS. LAW. We shall postpone that particular libation. The house is all that's left us after all. We shall resist its consummation.

MRS. ROBARTS. It is only wood and stone and trinkets and a few sticks of furniture and two grand chimneys that will stand up indistinguishable in this forest of chimneys. Not much in the course of things.

MRS. LAW. I think you misapprehend, Mary. It is everything.

MRS. ROBARTS. Au contraire, ma mere.

MRS. LAW. You have misapprehended a great deal this past day, I'm afraid, and that's the last I'll say about it. Now, let us make ready to greet the Reverend Mr. Robarts on his return. I'm afraid that God, in his infinite wisdom does not see fit for me to pass on today or tomorrow or next month, even. Ever obedient, I go on. Really, children, I think that this General Sherman doesn't amount to a hill of beans. No light is strewn here and there where he walks, is there, Mary? Kate, is there? Well, I can't be sure what either of you think, or what anybody thinks anymore, but we have our own business here and it is substantial, and we must be very competent. (*Pause.*) Mary, would you remember to take care of a little *pain et comfiture* for the Reverend Mr. Robarts? Kate dear, Mary, you have both had a spell of being fantastic. (*Pause.*) And a little brandy for the Reverend. I believe he is fond of the smallest amount to refresh him. There's a bottle in the boards above the kitchen closet. (*Pause.*) Otherwise, what can we do? (*She exits.*)

MRS. ROBARTS. Kate, listen, you will send us the most wonderful letters from Europe and I will send you the most wonderful letters about myself and my child or my many children and where I am and where I've been and where I intend to go. This war can't last, at least beyond next Tuesday.

KATE. Really?

MRS. ROBARTS. I think I'll go out for a minute, walk around. I need to leave this house.

KATE. I don't think you should.

MRS. ROBARTS. Here's something you can do. Set out some bread, if there is any, and a pitcher of coffee for Mr. Robarts. Just set it out and say I left it for him. I'll just be a moment.

KATE. Do you think so?

MRS. ROBARTS. And the brandy. He is fond of the smallest amount, he genuinely is. Would you? (*Pause.*) I want to say just a few more things about this. Excuse me. (*Exits.*)

KATE. Well, I'm not just going to wait here, Mary Robarts. I've had a taste of it too. You can take one of those horses if you want to, go ahead, though I think it is usually unwise for a woman expecting a child to be rushing here and there, but take it if you want and ride to Eden or New Place Station or Hopewell or beyond or wherever, but I think— O merde!

TUSSIE. It's like Fanny dreamed it in her visions. Hubert and Williams James and Nate all gone along with the soldiers, singing like fools, and Dan Josiah got so little humility he got him some crutches and a sling for his arm and a bandage for his head and he stood him by the road lookin' pretend hurt and he's never been sick a day in his life, let alone kilt, and so some man give him a hand up on a wagon. And Rhody and Abram, they just vanished from the earth. And Stella won't manage it through; and Andrew Dirt is so mad he run the other way to join Lee, he don't know where, totin' his old flint-lock, even though I said, you're black and you're carrying a gun and that means, Andrew Dirt, you're dead.

So there's Gramma Cealy and Maggie and Adeline, though she's simple-minded, and me. Miss Kate, we're gonna be free. How about that? Ain't that wonderful, to be free?

KATE. I don't know, and truth to tell, I don't care. You just see what we've got for the Reverend to eat and set out some strong waters—there's a bottle over the kitchen cupboard, set it out, and mind, none for you. I . . . I don't care where you went, Mary Robarts, I don't. But I know where I shall take a horse or two. (*Exits.*)

TUSSIE. (*Alone.*) She needn't said that to me. I never took anything that wasn't offered, not me. But that's not my concern, what she knows or doesn't know. (*Pause.*) It's bein' freed, that's my concern. My, won't that be nice? Oh yes, yes, sweet Jesus, won't that be something? (*Closes doors, exits. Blackout.*)

NOTE: When Sherman is quoted, it is Sherman. The Shakespeare in the third act is from *Henry V*. Mary Boykin Chestnut and the women whose letters are preserved in *Children of Pride* (New Haven, 1972) informed the consciousness of this play.

T.B.

PROPERTY LIST

5 teacups
5 saucers
Strike-anywhere matches
Taper
Key ring
Doiley
2 candles
2 candlesticks
Teapot
Creamer
Sugar bowl with sugar
5 spoons
Fork
Knife
13 plates
2 tier cake plate
Jelly sandwiches
Small oval basket
4 glasses
13 napkins
Metal tub
Crystal bowl
3 tea towels
Wicker basket with partitions
Brass tray
Wood tray
4 crystal glasses
2 decanters
9 stemmed glasses
8 pictures
Orange fabric
Break-away vase
Ball gown
Riding hat
Cloak
Urn
3 tin boxes
Bible
Statue

3 wicker baskets
Crystal pitcher
Apple
4 brandy bottles (one sealed)
Coffee tray
Tea tray
Coffee pot
Vase with rose
Shawl
Cane
2 lanterns with straps
Hand held lantern
4 saddlebags
Ledger
Chits
6 pencils
Blanket
Velvet fabric
Clipboard
Envelopes
5 pens
Requisition forms
Order papers
Pitch pipe
Small and large stationery
2 whiskey bottles (one full)
Rag
Humidor
5 cigars
Ashtray
Pounce Pot
Ink well
Memo
Full ink well
Roll blotter
Sealing wax
Seal
Sawdust
Crutch
Sofa map
Regimental flag
3 wall maps
Dummy map cases
Rectangular map case with 2 practical maps

Cigarettes
Surgeons' reports
Tied packet of letters (1 Hitchcock, 2 Strong)
Sealed envelopes for Sherman with 6 memos, news clipping, order
Message of Rev. Robarts' capture
Chicken
Penknife
Hammer
Table blotter
Blue cloth
Guitar
Cornbread
Mirror
Comb
Scissors
Razor
Peanuts
Pickle
Book
3 tri-fold orders of three
3 single tri-fold orders
2 jewel boxes
2 torches
Zoave rifle with bayonet
2 carbines
2 webbed belts
Scabbard
Strap with canteen and belt
Strap with canteen and bottle
Strap with food pouch
5 gun belts with ammo.
4 guns
2 swords
Blanket roll
Handkerchief
Violets
2 pocket watches
Hunting knife
Pipe
Tobacco

Furniture:
Sofa
Rug

Rocking chair
Table
Ottoman
5 crates
4 trunks
Upholstered chair
Highboy
5 dining chairs
Campaign desk
Campaign rocker
Campaign chair

Dressing:
Pink shawl
Black shawl
4 hat boxes
2 wooden boxes
Wicker suitcase
Metal box
2 sconces
Paisley fabric
Maroon velvet drape
3 rugs
Urn
Iron lamp
Brass lamp
Umbrella
Maroon fabric
2 file boxes

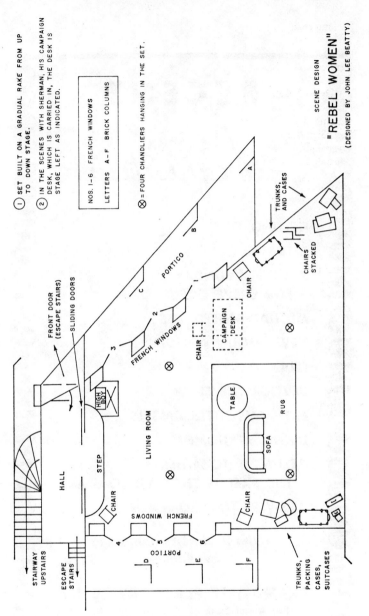

① SET BUILT ON A GRADUAL RAKE FROM UP TO DOWN STAGE.

② IN THE SCENES WITH SHERMAN, HIS CAMPAIGN DESK, WHICH IS CARRIED IN, THE DESK IS STAGE LEFT AS INDICATED.

NOS. 1-6   FRENCH WINDOWS

LETTERS A-F   BRICK COLUMNS

⊗ = FOUR CHANDLIERS HANGING IN THE SET.

SCENE DESIGN

"REBEL WOMEN"

(DESIGNED BY JOHN LEE BEATTY)

FRONT DOOR
(ESCAPE STAIRS)

SLIDING DOORS

PORTICO

A

B

C

TRUNKS, AND CASES

CHAIRS STACKED

CHAIR

CHAIR

CAMPAIGN DESK

FRENCH WINDOWS

2

3

HIGH BOY

LIVING ROOM

STEP

HALL

TABLE

SOFA

RUG

CHAIR

FRENCH WINDOWS

4

5

6

PORTICO

D

E

F

TRUNKS, PACKING CASES, SUITCASES

CHAIR

STAIRWAY UPSTAIRS

ESCAPE STAIRS

59

RECENT

Acquisitions

GETTING OUT

BETRAYAL

A LOVELY SUNDAY
   FOR CREVE COEUR

MUTUAL BENEFIT LIFE

NEVIS MOUNTAIN DEW

SEDUCED

DEVOUR THE SNOW

MOMMA'S LITTLE ANGELS

LIVING AT HOME

GETTIN' IT TOGETHER &
   THE PAST IS THE PAST (One Acts)

ANSWERS (Three One Acts)

*Write for information as to
availability*

DRAMATISTS PLAY SERVICE, Inc.

440 Park Avenue South   New York, N.Y. 10016

New

TITLES

BURIED CHILD

TALLEY'S FOLLY

ARTICHOKE

THE TENNIS GAME

SAY GOODNIGHT, GRACIE

OLD PHANTOMS

FAMILY BUSINESS

LATER

MASTERPIECES

THE NATURE AND PURPOSE
   OF THE UNIVERSE;
   DEATH COMES TO US ALL,
   MARY AGNES;
   'DENTITY CRISIS (One Acts)

• *Write for Information*

DRAMATISTS PLAY SERVICE, INC.

440 Park Avenue South   New York, N.Y. 10016

R0146818734 HUM   812
                      B113 7/00

HOUSTON PUBLIC LIBRARY

CENTRAL LIBRARY
500 MCKINNEY